Weekly Reader Book Club Presents

Knockout Knock Knocks

by
Caroline Anne Levine

illustrated by Giulio Maestro

E. P. DUTTON · NEW YORK

This book is a presentation of Newfield Publications, Inc. Newfield Publications offers book clubs for children from preschool through high school. For further information write to: **Newfield Publications, Inc.**, 4343 Equity Drive, Columbus, Ohio 43228.

Published by arrangement with Caroline Anne Levine and Giulio Maestro. Originally published by E. P. Dutton. Newfield Publications is a trademark of Newfield Publications, Inc. Weekly Reader is a federally registered trademark of Weekly Reader Corporation.

Library of Congress Cataloging in Publication Data

Levine, Caroline Anne.   Knockout knock knocks.

SUMMARY: Presents a collection of sixty-one jokes.
1. Knock-knock jokes.   2. Wit and humor, Juvenile.
[1. Jokes]   I. Maestro, Giulio.   II. Title.
PN6231.K55L4   1978   818'.5'407   78-6689
ISBN: 0-525-33255-3

Editor: Ann Troy   Designer: Giulio Maestro
Printed in the U.S.A.   First Edition

To Jerry

Knock, knock. —*Who's there?*

Otis. —*Otis who?*

Otis a wonderful day
for a ride in the park.

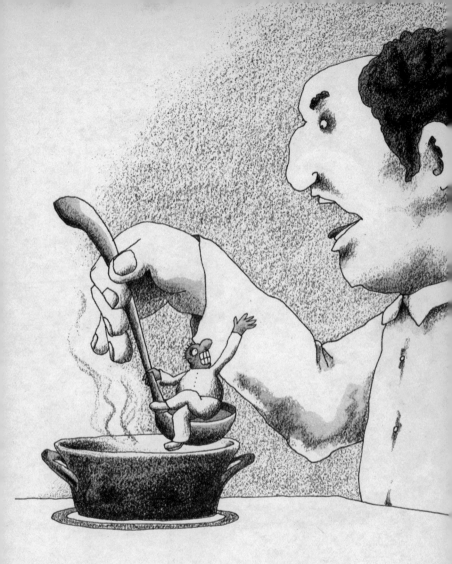

Knock, knock.   —*Who's there?*

Morris.   —*Morris who?*

Morris in the pot,
so help yourself.

Knock, knock.   —Who's there?

Dog.   —Dog who?

Doggone it, open the door.
It's snowing out here!

Knock, knock. —*Who's there?*

Alma. —*Alma who?*

Alma cookies are gone,
and I want some more!

Knock, knock.   —*Who's there?*

Beets.   —*Beets who?*

Beets me;
I just forgot my name!

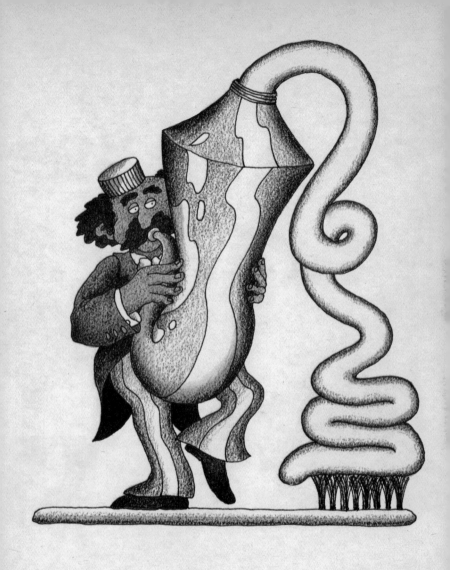

Knock, knock. —*Who's there?*

Tuba. —*Tuba who?*

Tuba toothpaste.

Knock, knock.   —*Who's there?*

José.   —*José who?*

"José can you see
by the dawn's early light?"

Knock, knock.   —*Who's there?*
Esther.   —*Esther who?*
Esther a bug in your ear?

Knock, knock.　—*Who's there?*

Isabel.　—*Isabel who?*

Isabel on your bike?

Knock, knock.   —*Who's there?*

Seth.   —*Seth who?*

Seth me. And what I seth, goes.
You hear?

Knock, knock.   —*Who's there?*
Hair.   —*Hair who?*
Hair today, gone tomorrow.

Knock, knock.   —*Who's there?*

Anna.   —*Anna who?*

Annanother thing . . .
How many times do I have to knock
before you answer the door?

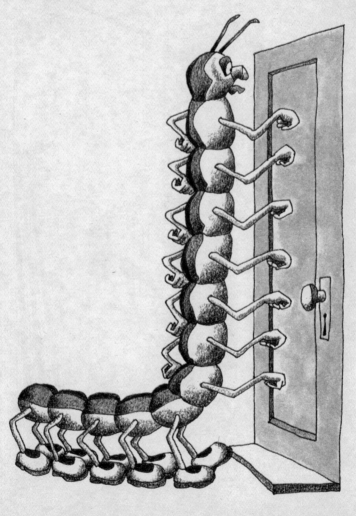

Knock, knock. —*Who's there?*

Todd. —*Todd who?*

Todd couple, that's who.

Knock, knock.   —*Who's there?*
Celia.   —*Celia who?*
Celia later, alligator!

Knock, knock.   —*Who's there?*

Gopher.   —*Gopher who?*

Gopher a touchdown,
rah rah!

Knock, knock. —*Who's there?*

Howard. —*Howard who?*

Howard is the ground when
you slip on a banana peel?

Knock, knock. —*Who's there?*
Shelby. —*Shelby who?*
"Shelby comin' round the mountain
when she comes. . . ."

Knock, knock.   —*Who's there?*

Henny.   —*Henny who?*

Henny Penny. I'm here to tell you the sky's falling in!

Knock, knock. —*Who's there?*

Kay. —*Kay who?*

Kay, L, M, N, O, P, Q, R, S,
T, U, V, W, X, Y and Z.

Knock, knock.   —*Who's there?*

Diesel.   —*Diesel who?*

Diesel be your last chance
to open the door!

Knock, knock.   —*Who's there?*

Emma.   —*Emma who?*

Emma pig when it comes
to ice cream!

Knock, knock. —*Who's there?*
Jess. —*Jess who?*
"Jess me and my shadow . . ."

Knock, knock.   —*Who's there?*

Lettuce.   —*Lettuce who?*

Lettuce tell you a few good
knock-knock jokes.

Knock, knock. —*Who's there?*

Eileen. —*Eileen who?*

Eileen'd on the fence too hard
and it broke.

Knock, knock.   —*Who's there?*

Catchup.   —*Catchup who?*

Catchup with me and I'll tell you.

Knock, knock. —*Who's there?*

Snow. —*Snow who?*

Snow use; I lost the little card
with my name on it.

Knock, knock. —*Who's there?*

Pizza. —*Pizza who?*

Pizza chocolate pie
would be great right now!

Knock, knock. —*Who's there?*

Iris. —*Iris who?*

Iristled for my dog.
Have you seen him?

Knock, knock. —*Who's there?*

Lee. —*Lee who?*

Lee me alone!
I have a headache.

Knock, knock.   —Who's there?

Robin.   —Robin who?

Robin the cookie jar is a "no-no."

Knock, knock. —*Who's there?*

Ken. —*Ken who?*

Ken I come in?
I'm freezing out here!

Knock, knock.   —*Who's there?*
Amos.   —*Amos who?*
Amosquito bit me! Ouch!

Knock, knock. —*Who's there?*

Romeo. —*Romeo who?*

Romeover to the other side
of the lake, and I'll tell you.

Knock, knock.   —*Who's there?*

Lion.   —*Lion who?*

Lion here on your doorstep
is no fun. Open up!

Knock, knock.   —*Who's there?*
Anteater.   —*Anteater who?*
Anteater whole jar of jam.

Knock, knock.   —*Who's there?*
Duane.   —*Duane who?*
Duane the bathtub. I'm dwowning!

Knock, knock.   —*Who's there?*

Cantaloupe.   —*Cantaloupe who?*

Cantaloupe until we get
the marriage license, honey.

Knock, knock.   —*Who's there?*

Philip.   —*Philip who?*

Philip this trick-or-treat bag
with lots of candy, please.

Knock, knock. —*Who's there?*

Butch. —*Butch who?*

"Butch your arms around me, honey,
   hold me tight . . ."

Knock, knock. —*Who's there?*
Canoe. —*Canoe who?*
Canoe come out and play?

Knock, knock.   —*Who's there?*

Ida.   —*Ida who?*

Ida know. Sorry.

Knock, knock. —*Who's there?*

You. —*You who?*

You-hoo! Anyone home?

Knock, knock. —*Who's there?*

Emile. —*Emile who?*

Emile fit for a king.

Knock, knock. —*Who's there?*

Little old lady. —*Little old lady who?*

I didn't know you could yodel!

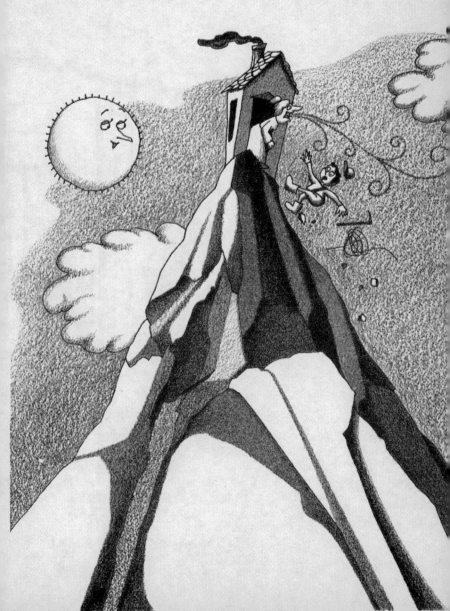

Knock, knock.   —*Who's there?*

Goose.   —*Goose who?*

Goose who's knocking at your door.

Knock, knock. —*Who's there?*

Hope. —*Hope who?*

Hopefully that present is for me!

Knock, knock. —*Who's there?*
Tarzan. —*Tarzan who?*
"Tarzan stripes forever."

Knock, knock.   —*Who's there?*

Piglet.   —*Piglet who?*

Piglet me in last time I came here.

Knock, knock. —*Who's there?*

Andrew. —*Andrew who?*

Andrew all over the wall, and is she in big trouble!

Knock, knock. —*Who's there?*

Banana. —*Banana who?*

Banana split, so Ice-creamed.

Knock, knock.   —Who's there?

Russia.   —Russia who?

Russia large salami-and-cheese
pizza to this address.

Knock, knock. —*Who's there?*

Izzie. —*Izzie who?*

Izzie at the door?
You'd better answer it.

Knock, knock.   —*Who's there?*
Owl.   —*Owl who?*
Owl I can say is "Knock, knock"!

Knock, knock.   —*Who's there?*

Lewis.   —*Lewis who?*

Lewis here on the porch waiting
for you to come out and play.

Knock, knock. —*Who's there?*
Olaf. —*Olaf who?*
Olaf, if you think it's that funny!

Knock, knock.   —*Who's there?*
Olive.   —*Olive who?*
Olive you, honeybunch!

Knock, knock.   —*Who's there?*

Cattle.   —*Cattle who?*

Cattle always purr
when you pet her.

Knock, knock.   —*Who's there?*
Ida.   —*Ida who?*
Ida baked a cake if Ida known
you were a comin'.

Knock, knock. —*Who's there?*

Arthur. —*Arthur who?*

Arthur any more brownies left?

Knock, knock.   —*Who's there?*
Welcome.   —*Welcome who?*
Welcome up and see me sometime.

Knock, knock. —*Who's there?*

Oliver. —*Oliver who?*

Oliver the place, people are
telling knock-knock jokes.